LIFE IN RELATION TO DEATH

Other books by Chagdud Tulku Rinpoche

Gates to Buddhist Practice
Lord of the Dance

Life in Relation to Death

SECOND EDITION

Chagdud Tulku Rinpoche

PADMA PUBLISHING

2000

Published by
Padma Publishing
P.O. Box 279
Junction City, CA 96048-0279

Printed in the United States of America
03   02   01   00   5   4   3   2

Library of Congress catalog card number:
99-044722

ISBN 1-881847-11-X

Contents

CONTENTS

Preface to
the First Edition

THIS BOOK IS BASED on a lecture given in Salem, Oregon, under the sponsorship of the Growth Place. Those who attended that lecture came from a variety of spiritual and intellectual disciplines to explore the topic of death from a Tibetan Buddhist perspective.

Every religion has its own teachings on the nature of death and its own methods for dealing with the death transition. My teachings come from an unbroken lineage of Buddhist meditation masters that extends back more than 2,500 years to Shakyamuni Buddha. The teachings of these masters have enduring relevance, because they are based on actual meditative insights into the passage of death and because they consistently relate death to life.

Buddhist masters see death not as an isolated event but as one more change in a never-ending cycle of changes. Those who hear Tibetan Buddhist teachings on death have the fortunate opportunity to learn to use their mind's power to direct these changes and to gain control over their lives—and over death. Death is a potent reminder to use life well.

The original lecture transcript has been reworked to clarify and expand certain points. A number of my students have helped in the preparation of this book, but special acknowledgment goes to Tsering Everest, who translated the original lecture.

Just as I hope that those at the lecture took home something of value that they could integrate into their own disciplines, so it is my heartfelt wish that you, likewise, will find this book useful in thinking about your life and preparing for your death. Beyond this, it is my wish that any positive influence these teachings may have on your mind expand outwardly as pure waves of compassion toward all others.

CHAGDUD TULKU RINPOCHE
Cottage Grove, Oregon
Spring 1987

Introduction

DEATH AND DYING is a subject that evokes such deep and disturbing emotions that we usually try to live in denial of death. Yet we could die tomorrow, completely unprepared and helpless. The time of death is uncertain but the truth of death is not. All who are born will certainly die.

People often make the mistake of being frivolous about death and think, "Oh, well, death happens to everybody. It's not a big deal, it's natural. I'll be fine."

This is a nice theory until one is dying. Then experience and theory differ. Then one is powerless and everything familiar is lost. One is overwhelmed by a great turbulence of fear, disorientation, and confusion. For this reason it is essential to prepare well in advance for the moment when the mind and body separate.

There are many methods, extraordinary and ordinary, to prepare for the transformation of death. The greatest of these results in enlightenment in one's lifetime. In enlightenment, death has no relevance to one's state of being. Enlightened realization is deathless, but it requires flawless meditative practice.

If deathless enlightenment is not accomplished during one's lifetime, the transition of death itself offers another supreme opportunity to attain enlightenment. But again, realizing the potential of this opportunity depends on having mastered certain meditative skills.

Enlightenment is the highest attainment of the death transition, but it is not the only one. If meditative realization is incomplete yet one has developed the power of prayer, there can be liberation into an environment of perfect bliss, free of suffering, by invoking the blessings of enlightened wisdom beings.

To accomplish the meditative skills and power needed to direct our mind at death, we must learn about the relationship of life and death, about the process of dying, and about the transitions from the moment of death until rebirth. In this way we become familiar with death and are not caught by surprise as the process begins to unfold.

Warned of a hurricane, we don't wait until the storm pounds the shore before we start to prepare. Similarly, knowing death is looming offshore, we shouldn't wait until it overpowers us before developing the meditative skills necessary to achieve the great potential of the mind at the moment of death.

DEATH AS WELL AS BIRTH, sickness, and old age are the four basic afflictions of the human condition. They are obvious and inescapable, in our personal experience and the experiences of other people. Yet these four afflictions fall within the larger categories of suffering that are experienced by all beings, human and nonhuman alike.

One of the greatest sufferings of sentient beings is the pain they experience from not getting what they want—or getting what they think they want, then finding it is not enough or that it is not what they really want. These constant frustrations are intrinsic to the impermanent, changeable nature of cyclic existence.

Then there is suffering atop suffering, which means that no matter how bad it is, it can get worse. On the day you lose your wallet, your tooth begins to ache and you get a furious call from your boss. Or on a larger scale, countries plagued by famine are also wracked by war.

Suffering pervades cyclic existence like oil pervades sesame seeds. Like the oil, the complete pervasiveness of suffering is not always apparent, especially in phases when pleasure predominates and things seem to go well. Yet, just as oil becomes obvious when the hard little seeds are ground and pressed, so latent suffering is directly experienced when our layers of egotistic assumptions crack under the oppression of cyclic existence.

Why is it like this? The answer is that we are subject to karma, the inexorable law of cause and effect. The question that follows logically is: What causes karma? The root cause is the poisons of the mind. Our mind is basically confused, because we do not recognize its absolute nature. Lacking this understanding, we slip into an erroneous framework, which is duality.

INTRODUCTION

We first grasp at a "self" who perceives and an "object" that is perceived. Seeing the object, we define its size, shape, and color. Then we judge it: "It's pretty. It's ugly. I like it. I don't like it. It makes me happy. It makes me unhappy." Finally, we feel either attachment or aversion: "I want it. I don't want it." This is where suffering begins.

The Twofold Truth:
Relative and Absolute

OUR PERCEPTIONS OF SELF and object, and our vacillation between attachment and aversion, are dualistic processes that occur in the mind. They are from the very outset a fictitious mode of perception. Once this dualistic process comes into play, we swing from one confusion to another, endlessly. And so we suffer, endlessly.

All suffering really comes from not knowing our true nature and from attachment and aversion, which are by-products of our ignorance. Because of these poisons we further complicate the spiral of suffering by nonvirtuous actions, speech, and thoughts. This dualistic mentality produces relative truth. In order to understand this term, consider the example of going to bed at night. There you are, between your warm sheets. Everything is safe. There is no problem. But through your mind, you leave your waking experience and begin your dream experience.

That experience is no less real to you than your waking reality. The environment is solid. The people are really people. They smile at you or they frown at you. Whatever happens feels very real. If you win the lottery, you are ecstatic. You become concerned with finding places to bury your money. If someone is beating you, it hurts. If you taste sugar, it is sweet. But though the dream seems quite real, it is not real outside of the dream context. Similarly, our waking state is not real outside of its self-produced context.

From the day we were born until the day we die, our life experience is an ever-changing relative truth that we hold to be very real. It is not, however, absolutely real or permanent. This is very important to understand. When you wake up from your dream of life, there are no possessions, no relationships, no emotional dramas. All of your experiences, which seemed true, were not really true in the absolute sense.

The criterion we can use for understanding absolute truth is permanence. If something is permanent, it is true. If it is impermanent, it is not true, because it is going to disappear. It will soon be only a memory. Everything in our reality is only dreamlike imagery, which we hold to be true and meaningful because we are so involved in it. Our experience is a product of our fundamental delusion. If there were no poisons in our mind, our perception of reality would be different.

To wake us up so that we can see the illusory quality of our relative reality and understand our foundational absolute nature is the goal of the Buddhadharma. Otherwise we just continue to dream. Our dreaming can be pleasant or unpleasant, but it never stays the same. We are born, we get sick, we get old, we die, and we never awaken from delusion's dream.

A completely awakened state is enlightenment, the unwavering recognition of the absolute nature of our being. Absolute nature pervades everything and is separate from nothing, but we have gone so far on a tangent, so far into mind's dualistic delusion, that we have lost sight of what is absolute. We follow the tangent of relative truth and think that the absolute is somewhere else, at some different time. Seeing separateness where there is none, we suffer in our experience of relative truth and in our longing for an unchanging, deathless absolute.

In a spiritual sense it is not very effective to attempt to change the outside world in order to prevent our own suffering. For example, if we glance into a mirror and see a dirty face we might think, "Oh, what a dirty face!" Then we quickly grab a cloth and scrub the mirror. This is not the way to get rid of the dirty face we see. Once we realize that the reflection is our own face, we can change the appearance in the mirror by simply washing our face. It will not work to wash away the suffering of our circumstances, but by recognizing our mind as the original cause we can change ourselves.

People see things in different ways. For instance, one man eats chili and he loves it so much that were he deprived of it, there would be little left worth eating. But another man eats chili and chokes in pain. The substance itself is not different. The habitual tendencies of perception, experience, and reaction are different.

So it is with life. One person sees things in a certain way, and another person sees the same things in an altogether different way. One man considered to be wonderful by his friends may be thought a brute by others. Yet the man is no different. The man is simply the man. Substance is simply substance. The world is simply the world. But we perceive and interact with it according to our own level of understanding.

Karma and Death

THE POISONS OF THE MIND create the karmic experience to which each being is subject. These poisons cause different perceptions of reality to arise, and consequently, sentient beings are found in one of the six major karmic realms, of which the human realm is one. Furthermore, within each realm every sentient being's karmic condition is unique according to the complexity of the poisons affecting the individual's mind.

For example, consider the common substance water. By perceiving water through the eyes of the beings of each of the six realms of karmic condition, we can understand how each being's experience is directly qualified by its own perceptions. The worldly gods perceive water as a divine substance, a bliss-producing nectar, quite different from the perception of humans and many animals that water is a very necessary, yet ordinary part of life. To other animals such as fish, water is the sustaining environment. Hungry ghosts perceive water as vile and disgusting pus, blood, and urine. To hell beings, water appears as molten lava, searing and terrifying.

The fortunate karma to be born into the high realms of worldly gods or humans is the result of virtue, but virtue that is mixed with attachment and aversion. Because of these two poisons, even beings of the high realms swing back and forth between hope and fear, and unchanging happiness is impossible to attain. In the high realms, just as in the lower realms, life has an impermanent quality.

The great catalyst for our hopes and fears is death. We need to understand that our life span will be only as long as our accumulation of positive karma supports it within the natural limits of human rebirth. If premature death threatens or interrupts our life span, this is because of negative karma created by past actions. We cannot know when such karma might arise, which is one reason for our fear of sudden death.

The karma of killing in a past life is a cause of premature death. The nonvirtue is so strong that it directly creates the experience of hell. However, once this nonvirtuous karma is exhausted by the hell experience, one can be reborn into the human realm, but one's life may be very short. Compassionate intervention to save the lives of others is the antidote to this danger of short life.

Compassion is founded upon the understanding that no one wants to die; everyone values his or her own life. When we save a life out of compassion for another being, we are engaging the power of body, speech, and mind to do something for someone else. This purifies negative karma and corrects habitual self-interest. It also develops our qualities as a compassionate being. When saving another's life, we can increase the benefit of our action with the wish that all beings without exception become free of suffering and come to know the unchanging bliss of enlightenment.

Therefore, our compassionate wish has two aspects—to stop immediate suffering and ultimately to benefit all beings throughout space, no matter who or where they are. By the quality of this twofold compassion, we create very potent virtue, which cleanses the mindstream. This is the direct method for overcoming all suffering and breaking through hope and fear. Ultimately it leads to complete release into the open simplicity of the absolute nature of mind.

The Dying Process

THERE COMES A POINT when it is obvious that death is near and cannot be turned back. Neither medicines, meditation methods that strengthen our elemental constitution, nor prayers will extend our life. Whether by degenerative disease or the completion of old age, we know that we will soon die.

An understanding of the physical, perceptual, and mental phenomena of the dying process may be very helpful as our own death approaches; it may also provide insights into the experiences of others who are dying. We should realize, however, that the strange sensations of dying and the loss of the familiar support of the body will still be very difficult. For this reason we must develop an unwavering recognition of the absolute nature that will carry us through the dying transition no matter what arises.

Dying begins when the five vital winds that sustain the body's functions and the five secondary winds that sustain the senses lose power, causing their functions to fail with them. In a complex interrelationship, the energy centers of the body, known as the chakras, begin to fail. As the energy of each chakra disperses, a corresponding element of the body—earth, water, fire, wind—also disperses.

These elements have a direct relationship to the body's components. The earth element relates to flesh and bone, the water element to blood and fluids, the fire element to digestion and internal heat, and the wind element to breath and circulation. When these elements dissociate, one after another, their cohesion and function deteriorate. The physical, mental, and visionary experiences of dying rapidly accelerate.

The first effects of dying are difficulty in digesting food, swallowing, and lifting the arms, legs, and head. The breath is short and gasping. The limbs, then the whole body, are chilled and nothing warms them. The mind is agitated and thoughts arise uncontrollably.

It becomes impossible to stay erect. We cannot lift our arms and legs, the head lolls back, and there is a feeling of heavy pressure on the whole body. The agitation ceases and is replaced by drowsiness, a semi-swoon. We see mirage-like visions and flickering lights.

There is dryness of mouth, nose, throat, and eyes. Bodily sensations are greatly reduced, and alternate between pain and pleasure, heat and cold. The mind becomes irritable and we have visions of smoke.

Then we cannot recognize friends or family. Sound and sight are confused. We see red dots like fireflies.

We become totally immobile. The breath is shorter and more gasping, our exhalations longer. Sound and sight blur. Visionary experiences arise according to our karma. Persons whose activities of body, speech, and mind have been very negative may see terrifying forms or a replay of the bad moments of their lives. They may react with guttural sounds of fear. Those who have been virtuous and kind may experience blissful, heavenly visions and see forms of loving friends and enlightened beings. They will have little fear of death.

Finally, there is one long exhalation, the "death rattle." This is followed by the closure of sight, hearing, smell, taste, and touch as the winds retract toward the heart. Physically one is dead.

NOTHING COMPARES TO the fear of death, not the anxiety of having a business fail, not the grief of loved ones dying, nothing. When we know death is imminent, there is fear far beyond any emotion we have experienced in our lives. Fear alternates with regret over the pointlessness of life. We worked hard and tried to be successful, but what do we have to show for our efforts? A terrible sadness arises if we look back and find that life was unfulfilling and rather meaningless.

Not knowing what will happen or where we will go, we feel deeply disturbed. Overwhelmed by emotions, we are powerless to deal with our confusion.

Our understanding of the dying process and the difficulties it involves should be an incentive to prepare for death. We begin this preparation by recognizing the dreamlike nature of our life. Moment by moment, we should look at life as if it were a dream unfolding. Whether we are putting gas in the car, washing the dishes, or taking a walk, we should stand back a bit and look at the situation, the dreamlike quality of it.

In this way we learn to accept that life will inevitably change, and we come to know that it is no more than one dream changing into another. By holding this view we create a slightly different stance in life, and our attachment diminishes. Things don't seem quite so solid, and we don't grasp at them so rigidly.

In this relaxed, more open state of being we have the opportunity to gain the infallible means for dying well, which is recognition of our absolute nature.

Daily Meditation
on Death

AT NIGHT when you can drop the activities of the day, you should engage in a series of meditative contemplations similar to these:

"All right, soon I'm going to fall asleep. How many people have I heard about who went to sleep and never woke up? When I lay my head down on my pillow, I may not wake up again. Death is not that complicated. It is simply a matter of not being able to take in one more breath. Then I am dead. That could happen to me tonight in my sleep."

Then critically and honestly look at your life and think, "If I die tonight in my sleep, what did I do with my day? What have I done with my life? Have I been of benefit or have I caused harm?" Sometimes it is not so pleasant to see how self-centered and selfish you have been, how focused on "me, my, mine." Whenever this has been the case, you have created karma that ultimately propels the mind in a difficult direction at the time of death. It is like forward motion. If you put something into motion, it continues to go that way. If your mind has been moving along a negative course, when you die it continues exactly the way it has been going all along.

So each night you should assess the general and specific direction of your life. You must recognize where you have indulged in the faults of your mind and harmed others. This negative karma must be purified, which means you must confess your faults before the wisdom being who is your object of spiritual commitment and devotion. You should take refuge in a perfect wisdom being, without any fault, the absolute expression of enlightened mind.

Begin by confessing, "I did it again. I have hurt others. I have caused harm. I have been wrong. I know better, but mistakenly I have done it again." Then accept absolution from whomever you know to be a perfect wisdom being. If, for example, you have faith in Jesus as your object of wisdom, visualize that blessings descend from him in the form of light or nectar and actually wash away your accumulation of nonvirtuous karma and negative mental habits.

Then, with the wisdom being as your witness, reaffirm your intention to benefit other beings by vowing, "I will help others in whatever way I can until I truly have the enlightened strength to bring them perfect bliss and happiness."

As important as it is to recognize your mistakes, it is equally important to recognize where you have been kind and where your activities of body, speech, and mind have been of benefit. The virtue of such activities creates merit that you dedicate generously with a pure, selfless heart to the immediate and ultimate benefit of all beings: "By the power of this dedication may each being find happiness and may all without exception attain the qualities of their intrinsic buddha nature."

With this, rest in the thought: "I have purified my karma. I have committed myself to selfless work for the benefit of others. I have dedicated my accumulation of merit to their happiness. Now if I die tonight I will have no regrets."

Having reflected on the day in this way,

meditate on your own death. Imagine that you are really going to die, that you actually enter death's passage and there is no way back. Imagine vividly different scenarios—an airplane crash, an automobile accident, terminal illness, stabbing by a mugger. Use your power of mind to make the event immediate and real. Any scenario you choose has some possibility, because you really do not know where and when your death might occur.

People often express fear about this kind of meditation and say, "If I think this way, maybe it will happen to me." But think of all the things that have ever crossed your mind— you would not have time in an eon for that many things to happen to you. Thinking about death is not going to make it happen, but it does prepare your mind for the death experience. So, courageously, imagine the details of your death as clearly as possible:

"There is a stabbing pain in my chest. It's my heart! I'm having a heart attack!

"I hear the ambulance sirens. I am placed on a stretcher, my wife is crying, and the dog is frantic. The paramedics trip on the stairs as they carry me out. The ambulance lights, the chaos, the bright lights of the emergency room . . .

"I overhear the doctor say, 'I am sorry, Mrs. Jones, but he's in pretty bad condition. We may not be able to pull him out of it.'

"My wife looks at me, stunned and brokenhearted. She's my last link. I can't say anything. I can't see her now. I'm so lonely, helpless . . .

"I am dying, but everyone dies. My life feels like a dream, and now it's going to end. Death feels very familiar. I know I've been through it before. Life, death—they are transitions I must make. What choice I have lies in the intention of my prayer, the power of my meditation, and the decision to use my spiritual connection to the wisdom being in whom I have faith."

With your mind and your heart, offer all that has been positive in your life to the benefit of every other being. Do not cling to anything. With the wisdom being who is your spiritual refuge as witness, say this heartfelt prayer:

"By the virtue I have accumulated in my life, may I and every other being who passes through the door of death find rebirth in a state of pure, sacred awareness."

Then allow your consciousness to merge into the heart of flawless wisdom. This completes the second phase of meditation.

Finally, in concluding the night's meditation on death, recall impermanence and the suffering it brings to all beings, and let compassion expand from the most profound depths of your heart-mind.

Suffering is so pervasive in our world, in all realms of existence, that there seems little we can do. Who has not been frustrated in trying to help even one person? How can we think of meeting the needs of the countless beings who are lost in the ocean of suffering? Only an enlightened wisdom being can truly benefit all beings, just as the radiance of the sun shines for all who stand in its light. With this thought aspire to enlightenment:

"From now until enlightenment, I will work ceaselessly for the welfare of others. In each moment I vow to reduce my faults and increase my qualities of compassion and wisdom. By following this spiritual path and the merit it generates, may I and all others find freedom from suffering and realize our innate enlightened potential."

Then drop all activities of the mind and relax. This relaxation is like the openness that occurs after the last thought passes and before the next one arises. The mind remains as the mind is, not unconscious, not dull, not analytical, just naked in open awareness. Let the mind rest there.

The Transition from Death to Rebirth

WHEN DEATH IS NEAR, the body's elemental constitution dissociates, and so begins the ending of life. Death leads to the intermediate state between death and rebirth, called "bardo" in Tibetan.

At birth the seed of masculine energy abides in the crown chakra. At death, when the elements weaken, the ascending wind can no longer hold this energy at the crown, and it begins its descent through the central channel to the heart center. At this time all thoughts arising from anger cease.

At birth the seed of feminine energy abides at the navel chakra. When the descending wind ceases to function, this energy begins to rise through the central channel. All thoughts arising from desire cease.

When these two energies meet at the heart, all thoughts arising from ignorance cease. There is no longer any stirring of poisonous thoughts. One swoons into a period of unconsciousness, then reawakens to the experience of mind just as mind is.

This reawakening is called the "clear-light bardo." If you have been a very great practitioner in your life and have mastered meditative skills in letting the mind be as it is, upon the dawning of the clear-light bardo the fruition of your meditative experience is recognition of the ground of absolute truth. This is called full enlightenment at the moment of death.

If you lack this profound meditative skill, the moment passes, then suddenly you apprehend color. The expression of the qualities of the natural mind appears as colors that form the different shapes of deities, both peaceful and wrathful. If in your life you have had the meditative skill to recognize the forms of the deities as the natural appearance of your mind, you can attain enlightenment at this stage of the bardo experience.

If you pass through both of these bardo stages without recognizing them as the expression of the absolute nature of your own mind and its pure qualities, you enter the "bardo of becoming," or "sidpa bardo." This is the beginning of the karmic route to ordinary rebirth. The tendency toward self-clinging, residual in the earlier bardo stages, expands into full-fledged dualism in the bardo of becoming.

In the bardo of becoming the experience of negative karma is intense, because the mind no longer has the stabilizing effect of a corporeal body. Inhabiting a mental body, your consciousness is confronted by terrifying hallucinations, horrible sounds, and nightmarish feelings of being blown about helplessly.

However, if in life you have fostered the practice of praying when things were beyond hope, prayer will be a natural reaction within the intensity of the bardo of becoming. Since the mind is not limited by an ordinary physical body, the instant you pray to a wisdom being the mind will be liberated into the environment of that being's wisdom awareness, which is free of any trace of suffering and is complete with the perfect qualities of enlightenment.

In summary, it is best to have realized the

nature of the mind through meditation, so that at the time of death, your consciousness merges inseparably with the fundamental ground of being. This is enlightenment.

Next best is to recognize that the appearance of divine forms is none other than the natural display of the ground of absolute truth, inseparable from the wisdom display of your own absolute nature. This likewise is enlightenment.

Finally, even without the meditative skills to become enlightened in the bardo, you can surely accomplish the power of prayer. This power comes from deep faith in the wisdom being who is the source of your spiritual refuge.

Sometimes prayer doesn't seem effective during one's life, because circumstances don't easily change according to one's wishes. However, in the bardo of becoming, the power of prayer is unobstructed and liberates one directly from the turmoil of suffering into an environment of infinite purity and bliss.

P'howa: Transference of Consciousness at the Moment of Death

TIBETAN BUDDHIST MEDITATORS have a special method of transferring consciousness into an environment of enlightened awareness at the moment of death. By successfully practicing this method, known as "p'howa," one bypasses the karmic destiny one faces in the bardo of becoming.

Although there are several categories of p'howa, the practice used to transfer consciousness at death is called the "p'howa of the three recognitions": recognition of one's central channel as the path, one's consciousness as the traveler on the path, and an environment of pure wisdom awareness as the destination.

Meditation instructions for p'howa are given within the context of death and dying teachings, then practiced repeatedly. With concentrated practice in the presence of a p'howa master, one can accomplish the skills of p'howa in several days. If one is practicing alone, accomplishment may take some weeks. However, compared with other kinds of meditation, which may require years of practice before unwavering realization is gained, p'howa gives very swift, sure results. One gains confidence and practical ability in the face of death.

The great result of p'howa accomplishment is liberation from cyclic rebirth and suffering.

Conclusion

THIS TEACHING ON DEATH and dying can reach into profound places in your understanding. Each crucial point is here. All you must do is listen fully, contemplate the meaning, and meditate until realization is accomplished in your mind.

Again, do not ignore impermanence. Whatever seems to be a priority in your life is really quite temporary. It comes and goes. Nothing is reliable.

We were born alone and naked. As our life unfolds we go through all manner of antics: needing, having, losing, suffering, crying, trying . . . but then we die, and we die alone. It does not make any difference whether we are rich or poor, known or unknown. Death is the great leveler. In a cemetery all corpses are alike.

Our relationships with one another are like the chance meeting of two strangers in a parking lot. They look at each other and smile. That is all there is between them. They leave and never see each other again. That is what life is—just a moment, a meeting, a passing, and then it is gone.

If you understand this, there is no time to fight. There is no time to argue. There is no time to hurt one another. Whether you think about it in terms of humanity, nations, communities, or individuals, there is no time for anything less than truly appreciating the brief interaction we have with one another.

Our worldly priorities can be ironic. We place first what we think we want most; then we discover that our wanting is insatiable. Paying off the house, writing the book, making the business successful, setting up the retirement, taking the big trip—things that are temporarily on top of our list of priorities completely consume our time and energy. And then at the end of life, we look back and wonder what all those things meant.

It is like someone who travels in a foreign country and pays his way in that country's currency. Then he gets to the border and is surprised to learn that the country's currency can't be exchanged or carried across. Like that, our worldly possessions and achievements cannot be carried through the portal of death. If we rely on them, we will find ourselves suddenly impoverished and bereft. The only currency that has any value when we travel across the threshold of death is our spiritual attainment.

It is better to develop contentment and appreciate what we have in a worldly sense. Time is very precious. Do not wait until you are dying to understand your spiritual nature. If you do it now, you will discover resources of kindness and compassion you didn't know you had. It is from this mind of intrinsic wisdom and compassion that you can truly benefit others.

Spiritual development begins with the resolve never to harm others. So, please, be careful. If you put yourself in another's place, you realize how destructive it is to hurt or kill another, even an insect. Life is life, and every being wants to live. If you hold others in this regard, you will close the door to your own suffering.

Mind is like a microscope. It magnifies

everything. If you criticize yourself all the time—"I am so poor, I am not tall enough, my nose is too big"—if you concentrate your attention on all your inadequacies and miseries, they will just get worse until you are ready to give up in despair.

Instead of saying, "I feel rotten. What should I do?" think of the suffering of others and generate compassion. It is very important to really see suffering, to pay attention to the harassed teller in the bank, the tired and pale old man shuffling down the street, the child crying miserably. See the depth of suffering and get a perspective on your own suffering. Others are sick, they are plagued by war and famine, they are dying.

Compassion is the fervent wish that all beings without exception, your worst enemy as well as your friend, find freedom from suffering. To develop genuine, all-inclusive compassion, first exercise compassion on those nearest you; then extend it to strangers and ultimately to all beings throughout space.

Then turn your wish toward their happiness. Since happiness comes only from virtue, wish that whatever happiness others have gained from their past virtue may never be di-

minished or lost, and that it may always increase until they gain infinite and unchanging
happiness. This wish for others' happiness is
what is truly meant by love. Rejoicing in whatever measure of happiness others have brings
limitless joy to our own existence.

Always recognize the dreamlike qualities
of life and reduce attachment and aversion.
Practice good-heartedness toward all beings.
Be loving and compassionate, no matter what
others do to you. What they do will not matter so much when you see it as a dream. The
trick is to have positive intention during the
dream. This is the essential point. This is true
spirituality.

If you wear robes, shave your head, pray
on your knees every day, and yet become
more angry, proud, righteous, and hard to get
along with, you are not practicing spirituality. You must practice the essence, which is
selfless love and compassion, and then try to
help others to the greatest extent of your ability. Use all your resources of body, speech,
and mind. This is the method. Whether you
are a Christian, Hindu, Jew, or Buddhist, love
and compassion are the same.

Victory over faults and delusion leads to

victory over death. My wish for each of you is that you attain all qualities of compassion and wisdom and the ultimate deathless state of enlightenment.

Afterword to
the Second Edition

SINCE ITS ORIGINAL publication in 1987,
this book has fulfilled the wish of His Emi-
nence Chagdud Tulku Rinpoche that it provide brief but profound instructions on preparing for death. Because it is short and
accessible, it has been read by a wide range of
people, many of whom have commented that
it is a book they feel comfortable giving to
their elderly parents or to friends who are
dealing with life-threatening illnesses.

A rich array of literature about the transitions of death is now available from Buddhists and teachers in other traditions, as well
as from hospice workers, counselors, and
memoir writers. *Life in Relation to Death*
maintains its place among these writings
by the practicality of its advice and by the
powerful, beneficial intention of Chagdud
Rinpoche.

The publication of this second edition created an opportunity to include some additional practical information. To that end, although the original text remains essentially unchanged, four appendixes containing sample documents have been added. The first is a Durable Power of Attorney for Health Care, the second a living will for life-support treatment, the third miscellaneous statements related to the two preceding documents, and the fourth a letter of instructions from a Buddhist practitioner regarding final arrangements.

Putting worldly affairs in order can be an important spiritual process. Writing a will enables us to look at our attachments and transform them into generosity. Our attachments will only obstruct us in the transitions of dying and death, whereas our legacies to relatives, friends, and charities will create merit that benefits us immensely in the afterdeath intermediate states and in future lifetimes. Having written a will, we should offer a dedication prayer that our wealth, possessions, virtue, and merit not only benefit those who receive them directly, but also enhance the prosperity and happiness of all beings in all realms of existence. Through the positive, selfless intention of this prayer, we increase the scope of our generosity tremendously.

Working through the decisions about life-support treatment in order to write a living will allows us to rehearse possible scenarios of dying and transform them into a powerful recognition of impermanence. Our compassion turns to those who die in a coma with their choices left unexpressed, helpless if their preferences are violated. Once we have written our instructions for life-support treatment, we can face the possibilities of the dying process—including medical emergencies or coma states—with greater confidence. We know we have done what we can, and even if our instructions were not followed precisely, it would not be because of our own lack of foresight.

Similarly, writing a letter of instructions for our final arrangements affords a special opportunity to relieve our loved ones of difficult decisions and to respond to their sorrow with forethought and compassion. As we think about what we need or would wish in order to die in peace, as we envision our own funeral, the persistent tendency to distance ourselves from death dissipates and we gain an invaluable measure of equanimity.

Chagdud Rinpoche has often been asked how arrangements for the deceased were handled in Tibet. Perhaps his description will serve as a starting point for thinking about our own final arrangements:

Except for tapping the crown of the head right after the last breath [to direct the consciousness upward], no one would touch the body of the deceased until a lama had transferred the consciousness with clear signs of accomplishment. The body would then be wrapped, but not cremated or otherwise destroyed, for three days. For forty-nine days after the time of death, special prayers and ceremonies would be performed. A different lama and his monks would come for one week at a time, for each of the seven weeks. Usually ten or fifteen monks would perform the ceremonies, but my own family used to sponsor death ceremonies with thirty-five monks participating.

These ceremonies involved a lot of expense for the monks' meals, offerings to the lamas, and ritual offerings. Offerings with requests for prayers would also be sent to various monasteries. Finally, on the forty-ninth day, a lama would conduct an elaborate ritual feast ceremony, then ignite a piece of paper inscribed with the name of the deceased. As the paper burned, the lama would look for indications as to where rebirth had taken place. Inauspicious signs meant that more prayers and ceremonies—often a hundred thousand recitations of the mantra of the Buddha Akshobhya—would be required.

For those who died an untimely death, which in Tibet meant between the ages of eighteen and fifty, a special *dur* ceremony would be performed to counteract any negative patterns that had brought about death. *Dur*s were not conducted for those who died before they reached eighteen unless an accident or, extremely rarely, a suicide had occurred. This was because death before adulthood was considered normal rather than a result of negative circumstances.

All this dharma activity and expense was willingly accepted by most families as a means to ensure that the deceased would reach a state of liberation or at least be reborn with a connection to the spiritual path. At the end of seven weeks of continuous prayers, the household members usually discovered that grief over their loss had been transformed into confidence that their loved one had received excellent guidance through the turbulence of the afterdeath intermediate states. They would continue to benefit the deceased by making offerings in his or her name at large monastic ceremonies and by making offerings to accomplished lamas and practitioners with requests for prayers. They would also dedicate the merit of their own virtuous actions and spiritual practice to the deceased.

However, Rinpoche has also said, "I know that much of this is not possible in Western countries, particularly for those who die in hospitals, and of course other religions have different death ceremonies." Yet the universal wisdom underlying some of these rituals cuts across traditions. For example, even if one has not been trained in p'howa, it is certainly beneficial at the time of one's death to visualize one's source of refuge above the crown of the head—whether that refuge is Buddha, Jesus Christ, or some other embodiment of enlightened wisdom—and to pray with faith for liberation.

Tapping the crown of the deceased's head

to direct the consciousness upward toward his or her source of refuge is thought to be extremely important by Buddhists and Hindus, and practitioners of other spiritual traditions might consider doing so if they feel intuitively that it might help. Likewise, the strong Tibetan Buddhist belief that the body should not be destroyed for three days may be relevant to other spiritual traditions. Those in the West who arrange death ceremonies have observed that preserving the body for a few days often helps friends and relatives of the deceased come to terms with the reality of death and work through their sense of loss.

In terms of ceremonies, it is most important to pray for the deceased according to one's own spiritual tradition on the first three days after death and on each seventh day for forty-nine days. Then, on the forty-ninth day, a group should meet to pray and share a feast during which substances such as food, drink, incense, flowers, and candles are offered to the source of spiritual refuge. Offering food after someone has died and organizing memorial services are common to many religions; the emphasis on specific days is unique to Tibetan Buddhism.

Offerings for the recitation of group prayers can be made to the congregation in one's spiritual tradition, tapping the power that resides in purely motivated spiritual assemblies. In many Chagdud Gonpa centers a list of names of the deceased is read aloud during morning meditation practice, and such lists are included in special death ceremonies performed several times a year. Other religious groups have similar prayer lists, as well as traditions of making contributions in memory of deceased friends and family members.

Finally, we should include the deceased in all of our dedication prayers so that again and again they will benefit across realms and across time from the merit of our virtuous actions and spiritual activities. This, more than copious tears and elaborate funerals, will well serve those who have passed through our lives into other states of being.

My wish joins Rinpoche's that *Life in Relation to Death* will find its audience not only in the English-speaking world, but also among those who speak Portuguese, Spanish, and German, languages into which it has been translated. I also hope that the appendixes added to this edition will inspire many readers to prepare a will, a living will, and instructions for final arrangements. With these documents in place, the challenge of death, whether it comes abruptly or over a more prolonged period, can be met with less unfinished business, fewer ordinary preoccupations. Then we will have more freedom to find mind's essence, its source, its liberation.

CHAGDUD KHADRO
Khadro Ling
Três Coroas, Brazil
Fall 1999

Appendixes:
Documenting Your Wishes

IN ADDITION TO A WILL apportioning your estate to your beneficiaries, three documents—a Durable Power of Attorney for Health Care, an Advance Directive for Health Care (living will), and a letter of instructions for final arrangements—should greatly facilitate carrying out your end-of-life wishes. The examples given here are a good starting point, having been written with considerable care and with reference to excellent source material.

The sources for the examples of the Durable Power of Attorney for Health Care and the Advance Directive for Health Care are primarily "Five Wishes," a form developed by an organization called Aging with Dignity based in Tallahassee, Florida,[1] and a well-

[1] Aging with Dignity, P.O. Box 1661, Tallahassee, FL, 32302-1661; *www.agingwithdignity.org*.

researched, succinct, and spiritually attuned book, *The Living Will*, by Joseph E. Beltran, D. Min.[2] It is recommended that you obtain these reference works if you wish to explore the issues further. You may want to use the "Five Wishes" form, which is somewhat more general than the examples here, because it meets the legal requirements in thirty-three states.[3]

Both sources recommend authorizing a health care agent and supplying him or her with an Advance Directive for Health Care rather than merely writing a living will. You should carefully select your health care agent as someone to whom you can talk openly about your values and who will do his or her best to incorporate them into your health care decisions. Although you may not choose a family member, certainly your agent should be capable of skillfully handling the strong

[2] Joseph E. Beltran, D. Min., *The Living Will and Other Life-and-Death Medical Choices,* Thomas Nelson Publishers, Nashville, 1994.
[3] Major states such as California and Texas are not among the thirty-three.

emotions and opinions of your relatives and friends, as well as the professional opinions of your medical personnel. It will be quite important that you not be ensnared in friction and conflict as you pass through the stages of dying and death and, if possible, that everyone involved have a sense of peace about your passing.

Be sure to discuss your Advance Directive for Health Care with your primary physician and to leave a copy, or at least instructions as to where a copy is located, attached to your medical records. It would be regrettable if, after all your efforts to create these documents, they gathered dust in a lost file at a time when you needed them!

The example of a letter of instructions is written by a Buddhist practitioner to her non-Buddhist friends and relatives. It is presented here only to inspire you to consider what arrangements would be most important to you and to urge you to write your own letter according to your own beliefs. It is also wonderful to include personal letters to your loved ones, especially to your children, in your death file. We often leave so much unsaid and feel such regret if death suddenly intervenes. A letter expressing our love and appreciation could be a legacy treasured above all others.

These sample documents are not meant to be used without appropriate legal and medical advice. It remains your responsibility to verify the specific requirements in your state or country pertaining to health care agents, witnesses, notarization, life-support regulations, and other issues. States and countries also vary widely in their regulations pertaining to death certificates and handling of the body. The author and the publisher accept no legal liability if problems result from the use of these forms.

That said, it is still hoped that these examples will clarify issues, as well as catalyze your effort to put your affairs in order and attain confidence in your life and in your death.

APPENDIX 1:
DURABLE POWER OF ATTORNEY
FOR HEALTH CARE

Note that different states have different requirements regarding who qualifies—and who does not qualify—as a health care agent. In general, your agent should be at least twenty-one years old; should not be your health care provider or the owner, the operator, or an employee of the health care facility serving you; should not be an agent for ten or more people unless such agent is your spouse or close relative.

I [YOUR NAME], _____

Residing at [ADDRESS] _____

Telephone _____

do hereby designate and appoint as my Health Care Agent:

Name _____

Phone Number _____

Address _____

City/State/Zip _____

If my Agent is not willing to make these choices for me, has divorced or legally separated from me, or has died, I choose (list your second and perhaps your third choice) as my Alternate Agent with the same authorizations:

[SECOND CHOICE]: Name _____

Phone Number _____

Address _____

City/State/Zip _____

[THIRD CHOICE]: Name _____

Phone Number _____

Address _____

City/State/Zip _____

My Agent is empowered to make health care decisions for me, subject to the limitations stated in this document, if I am unable to make such decisions for myself. My Agent's authority becomes effective if it is confirmed in writing by two physicians that I lack the capacity to make or to communicate informed health care decisions. My Agent is then to have the same authority to make health care decisions as I would if I had the capacity to make them, with reference to the Advance Directive for Health Care attached below. Photocopies of this Advance Directive shall have the same force and effect as the original.

Specifically, I authorize my Health Care Agent to do the following (cross out and initial those statements that you do *not* wish to authorize):

1. Make choices for me about my medical care or services, such as tests, medicine, life support, or surgery.

2. Stop treatments and services already started, including artificially provided food and fluids and other life-support treatments.

3. Interpret the health care instructions I have given previously.

4. Arrange admission to a hospital, hospice, or nursing home.

5. Hire or fire any health care worker.

6. See and approve release of my medical records and personal files.

7. Sign my name where required on such files.

8. Move me to another state if this is necessary for me to receive treatment according to my wishes and values.

9. Take any legal action needed to carry out my wishes.

10. Apply for Medicare, Medicaid, or other programs or insurance benefits for me. In order to fill out such forms, my Health Care Agent can examine my personal files, such as bank records, to obtain information.

11. Add any additional authorizations:

If I want to change my Health Care Agent, I will write "revoked" across the name of each agent whose authority I want to cancel and sign my name, or I will tell someone (or a specified number of persons) that I want to cancel or change my Health Care Agent.

DURABLE POWER OF ATTORNEY

I hereby authorize this Durable Power of Attorney for Health Care:

Your Signature _____

Date _____

Witness statements and/or notary public certification are required in some states. A sample witness statement can be found in Appendix 3.

Appendix 2:
Advance Directive for Health Care (Living Will)

I. Statement of fundamental values:

II. General instructions (cross out and rewrite if this statement does not express your views):

If I am unable to make my own health care decisions, I expect my doctors and my Health Care Agent to weigh the burdens and benefits of any form of medical treatment and recommend those treatments that provide an overall net gain—meaning the benefits are greater than the burdens—and are in my overall best interest *according to my values*. Because my Health Care Agent is more familiar with my values, I have authorized him or her to make such decisions.

Additions to the above statement or re-written statement:

III. Life support
  A. Choice of treatments (draw a line through and sign *each* life-support treatment you do *not* want):
    1. Tube feeding, that is, food and fluids supplied artificially by a medical device
       Sign and date here if you do *not* want tube feeding under any circumstances:

       _____

       List situations in which tube feeding *might* be acceptable to you and in which you authorize your Health Care Agent to accept tube feeding if he or she feels it is in your best interest:

    2. Medical devices inserted to help me breathe

3. Cardiopulmonary resuscitation (CPR)
4. Major surgery
5. Blood transfusions of blood products
6. Dialysis
7. Antibiotics

B. When I am close to death (choose *one* of the following options by circling the number):

1. I want life-support treatment (except those treatments I have indicated I do not want in Section III, A).

2. I want life-support treatment if my doctor believes it could help, but I want my doctor to stop giving me life-support treatment if it is not helping my health condition or symptoms. My Health Care Agent is authorized to make the final decision in this matter.

3. I do not want life-support treatment. If it has been started, I want it stopped.

C. If I am in a coma and I am not expected to wake up or recover (choose *one* of the following options by circling the number):

1. I want life-support treatment (except those treatments I have indicated I do not want in Section III, A).

2. I want life-support treatment if my doctor believes it could help, but I want my doctor to stop giving me life-support treatment if it is not helping my health condition or symptoms. My Health Care Agent is authorized to make the final decision in this matter.

3. I do not want life-support treatment. If it has been started, I want it stopped.

D. If I have permanent and severe brain damage or a chronic degenerative brain disease that makes me unable to recognize people and I am not expected to recover (choose *one* of the following options by circling the number):

1. I want life-support treatment (except those treatments I have indicated I do not want in Section III, A).

2. I want life-support treatment if my doctor believes it could help, but I want my doctor to stop giving me

life-support treatment if it is not helping my health condition or symptoms. My Health Care Agent is authorized to make the final decision in this matter.

3. I do not want life-support treatment. If it has been started, I want it stopped.

E. Other conditions under which I do *not* wish to be kept alive through life support (indicate by circling the number):

1. Intractable pain
2. Extreme dependence on others
3. Major financial depletion of my estate
4. List any other conditions:

IV. Palliative care

General statement: Although of course I want to be kept as clean and comfortable as possible, I do not want to impose extra legal duties on my health care providers, my Health Care Agent, or my friends and family through this statement of my wishes. I understand that they are not required by law to perform the care and tasks I have indicated, but I hope that they will respond compassionately to these requests (indicate the care you *do* want by circling the letter):

A. I want my doctor to give me enough medicine to relieve my pain, even if that means I will be drowsy or sleep more, *or*

B. I want pain alleviation, but because I believe that even in certain coma states important mental processes may be taking place, I am prepared to endure a measure of pain rather than substantially diminish mental clarity. I want my physician to discuss my situation and my options with my Health Care Agent and for them to decide together the appropriate pain relief treatment.

C. If I show signs of depression, nausea, shortness of breath, or hallucinations, I want my caregivers to do whatever they can to help me.

D. I want a cool, moist cloth put on my head if I have a fever.

E. I want my lips and mouth kept moist to stop dryness.

F. I want to have warm baths often. I wish to be kept fresh and clean at all times.

G. I want to be massaged with warm oils as often as possible.

H. I want to have personal care like shaving, nail clipping, hair brushing, and teeth brushing, as long as it does not cause me pain or discomfort.

I. If I am not able to control my bowel or bladder functions, I want my clothes and bed linens to be kept clean and to be changed as soon as they can be if they have been soiled.

J. I want to be offered food and fluids by mouth, and kept clean and warm.

V. Organ donation (indicate those statements that *do* apply by circling the letter):

A. I want to be an organ donor, *or*

B. I do not want to be an organ donor.

C. As an organ donor, once the activity of my brain decreases to the point that it does not support the vital functions of my body, I am willing to donate any organ or body part (including my heart, kidneys, and liver), even if it must be extracted while I am being maintained on life support.

D. Under no circumstances is life support acceptable to me. Therefore, I am willing to donate only such organs or body parts as can be extracted after death.

E. I am willing to donate my body for (indicate those statements that *do* apply by circling the number; all can be circled):
   1. Any purpose authorized by law
   2. Therapy of another person
   3. Medical education
   4. Transplantation
   5. Research
   6. My preference is:

F. Special conditions that must be met or religious practices that must be carried out before I am willing to donate my organs or body as indicated above (list the conditions or spiritual practices):

VI. Assisted suicide (cross out and rewrite if this statement does *not* express your views):

I do not wish to participate in assisted suicide because of my personal spiritual beliefs and because of the burden of moral and legal responsibility it would place on whoever undertook such assistance. Therefore, I do not want anything done by my health care personnel and caregivers with the direct intention of ending my life, even if their motivation is compassionate.

However, I also do not believe that withholding certain treatments (including tube feeding) or withdrawing them if they have been started constitutes assisted suicide *even if it leads indirectly to death*. For this reason I have entrusted my Health Care Agent to act on my behalf, in accordance with my values, to the best of his or her ability.

Additions to the above statement or rewritten statement:

VII. Special arrangements during my transition of dying (indicate those statements that *do* apply by circling the letter):

A. Choice of where you make the transition of dying (indicate your choice by circling the number):

1. I want to die at home if at all possible.
2. I want to die in a hospice.
3. I want to die in a hospital.
4. Other (state your preference):

B. I would like the following persons to be present when I die (list the relatives, friends, caregivers, and spiritual caregivers you wish to be present if possible):

C. I want to die with no one present if possible.
D. I wish to have others by my side praying for me whenever possible.

E. I wish to have the following notified that I am in the terminal stages of illness and asked to pray for me (list those to be notified):

F. I wish to have my favorite music played when possible until the time of my death (list the music):

G. I wish to have the following books, poems, and liturgies read aloud to me, even if I don't seem to respond (list your selections):

I hereby sign this Advance Directive for Health Care

_____

Date _____

Appendix 3:
Miscellaneous Statements

Witness Statement

Generally two witnesses are needed. Different states have different requirements as to who qualifies as a witness, so you should check your own state's requirements.

I declare that the person who signed or acknowledged these forms is personally known to me, that he/she signed or acknowledged this Durable Power of Attorney for Health Care and the Advance Directive for Health Care (living will) in my presence, and that he/she appears to be of sound mind and under no duress, fraud, or undue influence.

I also declare that I am over nineteen years of age and am *not:*

- the individual appointed as Health Care Agent or an Alternate Agent
- the person's health care provider or the owner or operator of a health care,

      long-term care, or other residential or community care facility serving the person

- an employee of the person's health care provider, of a facility serving the person's health care, or of his/her life insurance provider
- financially responsible for the person's health care
- related to the person by blood, marriage, or adoption
- to the best of my knowledge, a creditor of the person or entitled to any part of his/her estate under a will or codicil, by operation of law.

Signature of Witness 1 _____

Name [PRINT] _____

Phone Number(s) _____

Address _____

City/State/Zip _____

Signature of Witness 2 _____

Name [PRINT] _____

Phone Number(s) _____

Address _____

City/State/Zip _____

Notarization

In several states, including Hawaii, Missouri, and North Carolina, your signatures on the Durable Power of Attorney for Health Care and the Advance Directive for Health Care must be notarized with witnesses present. Even when not required, notarization reaffirms your clear intent with these documents.

Physician's Statement

The following statement likewise reaffirms your intent and strengthens the implementation of your Durable Power of Attorney for Health Care and your Advance Directive for Health Care. Remember that a copy of these documents, or at least a letter stating that you have such documents and noting who can be contacted in order to locate them, should be with your medical folder in the office of your primary physician.

I, the undersigned, am the physician of

_____.

I have seen this document and discussed it with _____.

If _____ becomes
unable to make competent decisions, I understand that it is my duty to be guided by this
Advance Directive for Health Care.

Signature _____

Date _____

Appendix 4:
Letter of Instructions

To my much-loved family and friends, instructions for the time of my death:

First of all, I want you to know how deeply I care for you. Our connection in this lifetime, especially our moments of affection and happiness, represent my great good fortune. The process of dying powerfully brings home the realization that as surely as we have come together we must separate and the time in between is all too brief. Of course I feel sorrow, but I also feel a sweet and intense appreciation for what we have shared.

As death approaches, however, any ordinary attachment I have for you will not help, since I am powerless to turn back from this journey. And your attachment to me, though very natural, will not be useful, because it may distract me and turn my attention to where I cannot really return—back to the circumstances of my life with you—and hinder me in the transition of death. What I need from you now is calmness, release, and the recognition that however my death appears outwardly, inwardly it is a profound spiritual opportunity. Your prayers, arising from your own depths of love and compassion, will certainly support me in my efforts to use this opportunity well.

You know that my spiritual training in recent years has been in Vajrayana Buddhism. The lineage masters of this tradition have left clear descriptions of what occurs at death and what meditative skills are needed to negotiate death's transition. Specifically, I have learned a technique called p'howa, or transference of consciousness at the moment of death. I have asked some Buddhist practitioners to be present at my death and assist me in the practice. They will help me sit up, if possible, and they will do the practice with me. They may also tap the top of my head, since the purpose of p'howa is to direct the consciousness out the crown of the head toward a destination of spiritual rebirth. P'howa does not involve any flamboyant ritual, and it does not take more than an hour or so. Hospitals are usually willing to create space and time for this meditation, especially if you discuss it with the staff ahead of time.

What follows is a checklist of instructions. I hope they are clear, because I may not be able to clarify them when I am closer to death, but if you have questions, you may ask my lama or any of my dharma friends whose names appear on the attached list.

1. Please notify my lama and dharma friends in time for them to be present before I die. Of course, it may be hard to tell when the actual moment of death will occur; if it somehow happens that they can't arrive in time, don't worry. The blessings of my spiritual training will support my passing.

2. Please do not touch my body, particularly my hands or feet, as death approaches, because your loving contact may draw my attention downward when my whole focus should be at the crown of my head.

3. If no other spiritual practitioner is present when I die, tap my skull in the center about eight fingerwidths back from my original hairline. This could be of immense benefit in channeling the exit of my consciousness.

4. It is best if my body is not handled much before the p'howa practice is finished. Cer-

tain signs occur when transference is successful, which other practitioners will recognize.
When the practice has been successful, it
doesn't matter at all what happens to my
corpse. I would prefer it to be cremated as in-
expensively as possible and the ashes used in
the making of tza-tsas, small sacred images
stamped out of clay. A lama can instruct you.
If tza-tsas prove too difficult to make, just
have my dharma friends scatter the ashes and
offer prayers. They are only ashes, the merest
residue of my life.

5. I am an organ donor, but I *do* want my
consciousness transferred before anyone
comes to harvest my organs. If for some reason this does not happen, don't worry: my
lama assures me that the merit of offering organs supersedes the disturbance to the body
and that my consciousness will be directed to
a high state of rebirth on the basis of that
merit.

6. There is a slight possibility that transference won't be achieved, my organs won't
be harvested, and my consciousness will re-
main lodged in my body for up to four days
and three nights. This will cause difficulties
for you, because my body should definitely

not be buried or cremated until the consciousness has exited—a lama can check to see if it has done so. In California and other states, you can keep the body as long as you have a death certificate and the body is properly refrigerated, but you can't bury or cremate it yourself. I don't want to burden you with my dead body (forgive me if many humorous possibilities spring to mind), but I want you to at least know about not destroying it prematurely. If you can't find a place to let it rest, then call the lamas and my dharma friends and urge them to practice p'howa. Performing p'howa successfully from a distance requires a very great meditator, so it would be best if they did the practice next to the body.

7. Please make offerings to the lamas who perform prayers and ceremonies after my death. I have designated a certain amount of money in my will for this purpose. I know I have not been the most virtuous person in this lifetime, and unless p'howa is successful and I take rebirth in a state beyond suffering and can purify my misdeeds there, I may be confronted after death with the full weight of my negative actions of body, speech, and

mind. This will definitely cause me suffering. You can alleviate this by asking my dharma friends to arrange for prayers to be said and for ceremonies to be conducted. Particularly, I want to sponsor a practitioner to recite the Akshobhya mantra and to create an image of that buddha. This will cost about $130 and can be facilitated through the Mahakaruna Foundation (P.O. Box 344, Junction City, CA 96048-0344). My lamas will suggest other ceremonies.

Thank you for all that you have done and will do. I know that it requires a certain tolerance to honor my spiritual belief system when it is different from your own, but I can hope that your respect for my requests will become a source of positive energy that will ease your mind at the time of your own death. According to the teachings I have received, if all goes well, after death I will find liberation from selfish concerns in the realms beyond death and will attain vastly enhanced abilities to benefit you and all beings. This is what I most wish. May it come about just so!

About the Author

CHAGDUD TULKU RINPOCHE was born in eastern Tibet in 1930, son of Delog Dawa Drolma, one of Tibet's most renowned female lamas. At age two he was recognized as abbot of Chagdud Gonpa, a centuries-old monastery and one of the few that would survive destruction by the Chinese Communists. He received extensive training from many great lamas and belongs to the last generation of teachers to have inherited the vast wealth of Vajrayana Buddhist teachings and methods while still living in Tibet.

In 1959 Rinpoche went into exile and, during the two decades that followed, served the Tibetan community in India and Nepal as lama and physician. At the request of H.H. Dudjom Rinpoche, he established a refugee camp in Orissa, India, which the Indian government considered to be a model of economic self-sufficiency. He was widely known for his ability to heal, and he trained many people in the technique of p'howa, the transference of consciousness at the moment of death.

In 1979, at the invitation of several American students, he came to the United States, first establishing his seat in Cottage Grove, Oregon, and later at Rigdzin Ling, in Junction City, California. He founded centers for the study and practice of Vajrayana Buddhism throughout the United States, as well as in Canada, Europe, and Brazil.

Since 1996, Chagdud Rinpoche has resided at his South American seat, called Khadro Ling, in Três Coroas, southern Brazil. Rinpoche is the author of two other books: *Gates to Buddhist Practice* and *Lord of the Dance,* his autobiography.